The Triumph
of Faith

Copyright © 2025 by Wiljean Compère

Published by Four Rivers Media

All rights reserved. No portion of this book may be reproduced, stored in a retrieval system, or transmitted in any form or by any means—electronic, mechanical, photocopy, recording, scanning, or other—except for brief quotations in critical reviews or articles, without prior written permission of the author.

Unless otherwise noted, all Scripture quotations are taken from the New King James Version®. Copyright © 1982 by Thomas Nelson. Used by permission. All rights reserved. | Scripture quotations marked NIV are taken from the Holy Bible, New International Version®, NIV®. Copyright © 1973, 1978, 1984, 2011 by Biblica, Inc.™ Used by permission of Zondervan. All rights reserved worldwide. www.zondervan.com. The "NIV" and "New International Version" are trademarks registered in the United States Patent and Trademark Office by Biblica, Inc.™ | Scripture quotations marked ESV are taken from The ESV® Bible (The Holy Bible, English Standard Version®), copyright © 2001 by Crossway, a publishing ministry of Good News Publishers. Used by permission. All rights reserved.

For foreign and subsidiary rights, contact the author.

Cover design by: Sara Young

ISBN: 978-1-962401-60-9   1 2 3 4 5 6 7 8 9 10

Printed in the United States of America

The Triumph of Faith

GOD HAS THE ABILITY TO MULTIPLY
50 CENTS IN INCALCULABLE QUANTITIES

WILJEAN COMPERE

*"I have set before you an open door,
which no one is able to shut."*
—*Revelation 3:8*

"All things are possible for one who believes."
—*Mark 9:23*

Contents

Preface ix

Introduction 13

CHAPTER 1. **My Conversion** 17

CHAPTER 2. **My Miraculous Healing** 23

CHAPTER 3. **My Calling and Vocation** 35

CHAPTER 4. **A Companion for Ministry and Family** . . . 63

CHAPTER 5. **The Impact of Open Door Ministry** 71

Conclusion. 85

Preface

This work, *The Triumph of Faith*, is the work of a great servant of God. It is the Reverend Pastor Wiljean Compère, President of the Open Door Bible Seminary and pastor of the Open Door Church of Cap-Haïtien, the second largest city and the historical and tourist capital of the Republic of Haiti. Rev. Compère also serves as the pastor of the First Open Door Church of Bois-de-Lance, a communal section of Limonade. He holds a Master's degree in Leadership and Ministry and is the President of the Open Door Mission Church in Haiti, which includes over thirty seven churches operating in the following governmental administrative divisions: the North, the Northeast, the Central Plateau, the Artibonite, and the West Departments.

Pastor Wiljean Compère is a man of faith, a hard worker, and a visionary. He is known and sought after for his talents and spirit of collaboration. The author of the work, *The Triumph of Faith*, wants to share with you, dear readers, his conversion, his faith, his consecration, his calling, his vocation, his ministry, his exploits, and his experiences with God. As a professor at the Open Door

Bible Seminary, Pastor Wiljean Compère continually works for the happiness of the institution by training Christian leaders for the flourishing of the saving gospel. His dynamism and dedication to the Master's cause have made him a discerning and responsible leader.

The Triumph of Faith highlights God's faithfulness, peace in suffering, and victory in trials. I sincerely hope that the readers of this work will be fully edified by the vibrant testimony of this great man of God whose ministerial life is the fruit of miracles. In our time, God is seeking servants who are able to experience His power, His mercy, His love, His deliverance, and His miracles. In every generation, God raises up tested men and women of faith. Even today, He longs for tender, confident, and submissive hearts for the construction of His kingdom. The time has come to let go of your worries, your despair, your setbacks, and your doubts to respond to God's call. Rev. Wiljean Compère, through his work, offers solutions to your problems and answers to your questions. He invites you to believe in Jesus, who has the power to bring healing to the sick, peace to troubled hearts, joy to saddened souls, hope to despairing friends, aid to the abandoned, and comfort to the weak.

The author, through his work, wants to present to you the One who has the ability to change circumstances. He is the Almighty God, the Incomparable. There is no one like Him, and nothing resembles His works. Distinguished friends in the Lord, may the reading of this work bless you and help you overcome your obstacles and navigate your path strewn with sorrow and trial. Note that the trial comes before promotion, knowing that your perseverance, your faith, your patience, and your courage will allow you to sing victory at the summit of the mountain.

Happy reading!

—Rev. Dr. Childéric Présumé
Pastor of the Evangelical Church of Haiti of Vertières, Cap-Haïtien
Professor at the Open Door Bible Seminary and Emmaus University

Introduction

The redemptive encounter of Jesus Christ with a weary and burdened person always brings divine transformation. It leads that person to receive Jesus Christ into their heart to be their Savior and Lord. And the beneficiary of this marvelous encounter cannot remain silent about the glory, for faith leads to contemplate the magnificence of God. The Samaritan woman, upon encountering Jesus Christ, had a transformative experience. And it placed before her a mission as a disciple of Jesus Christ, that of testifying for Christ. This testimony included a testimony centered on Christ and the testimony of her encounter with Christ (John 4).

A life changed by an encounter with Jesus Christ is a convincing message. This has great importance, and all of this is the manifestation of the Gospel of Christ, which is a divine power to save the believer in Christ (Romans 1:16). Jesus Christ was able to show that those who testify for Him before men will have their testimony with His Father at His glorious coming, but those who refuse to do so will not have access to this great privilege (Matthew 10:32-33). After the healing performed by Jesus Christ for a man who was tormented by demonic possession, he wanted to stay with Jesus Christ, but Jesus Christ ordered him to return home to tell of the blessings of God upon him (Luke 8:39). All of this shows how important it is to testify for Christ. Indeed, I want to mention the reasons why I am writing this book:

1) To recount the blessings of God in my favor in order to praise Him, for God healed my soul and body, and He opened a door before me that no one can shut.
2) To write it with the intention of making my experiences accessible to all. I hope it can help them in their walk with God in the valley of the shadow of death within their ministry and in life.
3) To fulfill the expectations of many who have eagerly awaited the writing of this book in order to read through its pages how God transformed me and opened a door for His humble servant who had only fifty cents, but that did not prevent God from using me to accomplish great works for His glory and for the advancement of His kingdom. All glory belongs to God alone!

Furthermore, the content of this book is composed of five chapters. The first chapter deals with my conversion. The second chapter highlights my miraculous healings performed by God. The third chapter emphasizes God's call to me and the vocation that God has granted to my humble personality. The fourth chapter highlights the necessity of a companion and the integration of my family into ministry, and the fifth chapter concludes the book with the impact of the Open Door ministry under the power of the triune

God. Therefore, I want my life to be a subject of glory to God. I no longer want to resist His blessed voice as before. To repeat the prophet Jeremiah: "O LORD, I know the way of man is not in himself; It is not in man who walks to direct his own steps" (Jeremiah 10:23).

CHAPTER 1

My Conversion

This part will be considered in three sections:

1) Definition of the term conversion.
2) Before my conversion.
3) During my conversion.

Before delving into the subject matter, let us attempt to find a meaning for the word conversion.

DEFINITION

The word conversion is a noun derived from the verb "to convert." This vocabulary can be translated into Greek by the New Testament word: *stréphomai*, meaning "to convert" (Matthew 18:3). It can be derived from the Greek word found in the Old Testament *espitrophê*, the action of turning around, of turning towards. The Bible clarifies the reality of conversion by stating:

> *You turned to God from idols to serve the living and true God, and to wait for His Son from heaven, whom He raised from the dead, even Jesus who delivers us from the wrath to come.* —1 Thessalonians 1:9-10

John MacArthur argued that people experiencing conversion to Christ rejected lifeless idolatrous practices to become willing slaves of the living God: "Conversion is a complete change of orientation, a turning of the whole being to the Lord."

BEFORE MY CONVERSION

It is written in the Bible: "And you *He made alive*, who were dead in trespasses and sins" (Ephesians 2:1). On the other hand, it is written: "For all have sinned and fall short of the glory of God" (Romans 3:23). Every human being is an heir of the Adamic nature. Consequently, we are all spiritually separated from God. We are all worthy of divine wrath, but through His beloved Son, He offers us forgiveness, reconciliation, and His great grace.

Before my encounter with Christ, my beloved Savior, I was lost. I was dead (Romans 6:23), but the saving grace of the living God freed me from the condemnation of sin and death and gave me a living hope in Christ (Romans 8:2; 6:23). I was born on April 12, 1965, into a non-Christian family, in the Centre department, in Cerca Carvajal, in the communal section of central Haiti. My family consists of seven children, including three boys and four girls. I am the eldest. My father's name was Jean Compère; he called me Wiljean Compère. My parents' livelihood was farming, and my parents could not leave me alone at home. They would take me to the garden from age two, leaving me on a small chair while they worked. While sitting on this small chair, I started working by pulling weeds with my hands. After a few years, I started planting seeds without knowing how to do it. But my father would help me by showing me how to do it. Later, I made my little garden with stones as a fence. I told my parents, "Stay in your garden; this is my garden." The love for farming was already ingrained in my heart.

With time, I became a ten-year-old boy, and the time for me to go to school had come. Since I was small and the school I had to attend was far away from me, with rivers to cross and mountains to climb, the journey was dangerous, especially during the rainy seasons. From my house to the location of the school I had to attend, it took two hours to walk there. For my parents, this was the ideal age for me to start my school life. I could take the road to school alone. Since there were all these difficulties that children and young people from my communal section had to face to go to school in search of the bread of education, God would allow me to establish a school and a church there. I will speak more about these two accomplishments. All glory belongs to God.

> **THERE IS ONLY ONE PERSON WHO CAN HEAL. THAT PERSON IS NONE OTHER THAN *JEHOVAH-RAPHA*.**

I started my school life very well. But, when I reached the sixth grade, I was struck by a terrible illness manifested by headaches. My parents took me to the hospital and the doctor's diagnosis revealed that I was suffering from Turner Syndrome. Despite my shaky health condition, I continued with my school life. Since my parents were Catholics, they had me enter the catechism class to receive my first communion. I ended up being communed, confirmed, and renewed. Then, I became a sacristan's assistant. I was very enthusiastic. But my health condition became more and more serious. In an attempt to relieve me from the illness, my parents went to contact voodoo priests, but the situation persisted. Nothing worked. Because there is only one person who can heal. That person is none other than *Jehovah-Rapha*, the Lord who could heal me. He declares: "Now see that I, *even* I, *am* He, And *there is* no God besides Me; I kill and I make alive; I wound and I heal; Nor *is there any* who can deliver from My hand" (Deuteronomy 32:39).

DURING MY CONVERSION

To speak of my conversion, I want to mention the words of R. Saillens "Great God, your sovereign grace," which Charles R. Swindoll included in his book titled *Paul the Courageous Apostle of Grace*:

Great God, your sovereign grace
Has deigned to come to me!
Your mercy surpasses
All that I knew of you;
To the praise of your grace
Rises the hymn of my faith!
Alas! In my extreme folly,
Lord, I did not seek you;
You deigned to seek me yourself,
Your grace shone on my steps. . . .
Now, O Father, I love you,
And I am happy in your arms.

The song of my heart or the song of my gratitude are words inserted in number 11 Creole of the collection *Chant d'Espérance*. As it is not copyrighted but is in the public domain, I want to mention a verse and its chorus:

Without Jesus, I cannot live,
I cannot take a single step;
It is He alone that I want to follow.
I follow Him until the end.
I have nothing to worry about,
Because my Savior is watching;
I will follow Him without ever complaining,
He will not let me drown.

The Holy Spirit, the Comforter par excellence, the Spirit of life in Jesus Christ, liberated me and convinced me through the message of His servant, Pastor Oclane Onézias. On October 8, 1986, when I was in the ninth grade, I received Jesus Christ into my life as my Savior and Lord! This pastor, leaving his community, came as a missionary to Lacienne. He evangelized, and subsequently, he founded a church. After some time, this church was struck by a terrible persecution that closed its doors. Twenty years later, God asked me to return quickly to Lacienne to refound this church whose doors had been closed. Said and done, this church was refounded, and it was still Pastor Oclane who took its leadership in July 2008.

As I successfully underwent the official exams of the ninth grade, I continued my studies. Upon arriving in Hinche, I chose a church to worship God in and nourish my soul. God directed me to the Church of God in Hinche. At that time, there was a forty-day fasting period taking place at this church. I participated from beginning to end in this spiritual activity. At the end of this fasting period, it was decided to baptize those who were destined for this purpose. So, I presented myself to die and rise with Christ symbolically by receiving baptism.

Thus, I was immersed in the waters of baptism by the late Pastor Énoc J. René at the Church of God in Hinche on December 11, 1986. After my baptism, I preached my first message, the passage of which was taken from the book of Revelation 2:4: "Nevertheless I have *this* against you, that you have left your first love." After this preaching, Pastor Énoc told me, "You are a pastor." For me, this did not come to mind. But I was still sick during this period, although not as before. God knew why. For the Bible affirms: "And we know that all things work together for good to those who love God, to those who are the called according to *His* purpose" (Romans 8:28).

CHAPTER 2

My Miraculous Healing

After my conversion, God performed miraculous things in my life. He allowed me to experience spiritual and physical healing. My miraculous healing can be seen from two perspectives: spiritually and physically, and it can have several facets. My healing was spiritual as I accepted Jesus Christ as my Savior and Lord, and physical through various divine means during moments of fervent prayer. So, I will further discuss this.

God is the God of wonders, the God of miracles. He healed Naaman of his leprosy, an incurable disease. He healed a man born blind; He gave Abraham a son in his old age—all these acts were done miraculously. It is written in the Bible: "Jesus Christ *is* the same yesterday, today, and forever" (Hebrews 13:8).

I lend the words of the psalmist to praise the name of my God, the Father of my Lord and Savior Jesus Christ, the God of healing:

Bless the LORD, O my soul; And all that is within me bless His holy name!

Bless the LORD, O my soul, And forget not all His benefits: Who forgives all your iniquities, Who heals all your diseases. —Psalm 103:1-3

SPIRITUAL HEALING

My spiritual healing can be explained by the change that the Holy Spirit brought about in my life when I found God's forgiveness by accepting Jesus Christ as my Savior and Lord. My life underwent a spiritual transformation.

> **GOD IS THE GOD OF WONDERS, THE GOD OF MIRACLES.**

Previously, I lived according to my own desires. I took part in various festivities. Through my political life, I dared to speak ill of God, seeing the church as an obstacle to social development. Since I did not know the living and true God, I agreed to consult mortal men (witch doctors) for alleged deliverance or healing.

However, God made me a new man, a new creation in Christ:

Therefore, if anyone is in Christ, he is a new creation; old things have passed away; behold, all things have become new. Now all things are of God, who has reconciled us to

> *Himself through Jesus Christ, and has given us the ministry of reconciliation. —2 Corinthians 5:17-18*

You who suffer under the bondage of sin, you whom the devil holds under his tyrannical domination, God can heal you from these diseases; He can give you liberation and rest. It is good that you respond to His voice of love that says to you, "Come to Me, all *you* who labor and are heavy laden, and I will give you rest" (Matthew 11:28). If you come to Christ for Him to be your Savior and Lord, you will be a redeemed person for the day of redemption; your soul and spirit will be healed.

Often, you and I think that the most important healing is that of our bodies. But God, through His powerful and living Word, shows that the healing of our soul and spirit is the most crucial. We receive spiritual healing by finding forgiveness for our sins that only God can grant us through faith in the sacrificial death of His only Son, Jesus Christ, through whom we can be justified.

Mark 2:3-12 puts us in contact with the healing of a paralytic who was the beneficiary of Jesus's intervention. People thought that Jesus was going to heal this man of his physical illness, which is why they brought this sick person to Jesus. This reason was not paramount for Jesus; it was not the fundamental reason.

Amidst the astonishment of the crowd, but motivated by the faith of the paralytic's carriers, Jesus said to the sick man: "Son, your sins are forgiven you" (Mark 2:5). The Greek word for forgive means "send away" or "drive away." That is why the psalmist, under the inspiration of the Holy Spirit, wrote: "As far as the east is from the west, *So* far has He removed our transgressions from us" (Psalm 103:12). The prophet Jeremiah, under the influence of the Spirit of life, continues to affirm: "I will forgive their iniquity, and their sin I will remember no more" (Jeremiah 31:34). Under the power of the Holy Comforter, the prophet Micah adds: "He will again have compassion on us; He will tread our iniquities underfoot. You will cast all our sins into the depths of the sea" (Micah 7:19).

For the Jews, disease and suffering were caused by sins committed. It is possible that this paralytic was influenced by this belief, and it could lead him to believe that for him to be healed of his illness, he must first receive forgiveness for his sins. Indeed, he was freed from the embarrassment of his sins and the guilt he carried by the grace of Jesus Christ, the Redeeming God. He applied to him, first and foremost, his spiritual healing.

JESUS CHRIST IS MY GOD-SAVIOR, MY TRUE LIFE, MY PERFECT HEALTH!

In the same way, Jesus Christ gave me spiritual healing and changed my life, my direction, and my goals by placing me in the body of Christ, in the plan of His kingdom, in order to make me capable of bearing fruits that can glorify the name of the God-Man, the Lamb who takes away the sin of humanity, the High Priest par excellence. Hallelujah! Jesus Christ is my God-Savior, my true life, my perfect health!

PHYSICAL HEALING

The Bible advises us to seek first the kingdom and righteousness of God; all these things will be given to us as well (Matthew 6:33). In order for us to enjoy the wonderful care and rich provisions of God, it is of great kindness that we experience a life regenerated, sanctified by the blood of Jesus Christ.

Indeed, Jesus the Crucified is the only means to find the free gift of God (Romans 6:23b) because "there is salvation in no one else, for there is no other name under heaven given among men by which we must be saved" (Acts 4:12). The child who is lost, injured in the streets, is not under the protection offered by the paternal home. For this to be possible, he must return to his father's house to be cared for in view of healing.

My physical healing was the result of the miraculous interventions of the God of Wonders, and this happened in several stages. I must say that I suffered from several illnesses. After periods of prayer with perseverance, God healed me.

The First Intervention

The first healing that was performed in my life by God was at the level of my stomach. Everything I ate caused constipation. I was unable to eat. There was nothing I ate that did not lead to this illness.

During an evangelical crusade organized by Evangelist Daniel in Port-au-Prince, while I was in Cerca Carvajal (I was listening through the radio), I applied my faith. In the night, I saw someone giving me a small bowl. He told me to drink three spoonsful, and I did as the person told me. This is how God healed me. And since then, I can eat any food I want, and everything is fine by the grace of God.

The Second Intervention

I suffered from headaches—one headache for four months. Doctors—witch doctors—could not heal me of this pain. For me to be healed, there was a pastor named Pastor Oclane Onezias; he fasted with me for twenty-one days and forty days. I also took part in prayer vigils. After a prayer vigil, God gave me a miraculous intervention. It was a healing intervention that delivered me from the headaches that were causing me bitter suffering.

I want to explain how this happened. After a prayer vigil—we know that a prayer vigil can last all night until morning; it can also happen at midnight, and at this hour, the participants can go to rest, and at 4 o'clock in the morning, they get up to say a last prayer just before returning to their home.

During this rest time, I was dozing off, and then, in a dream, I found myself in a hospital. I saw four doctors wearing white clothes; they were opening my head, and there was a lot of blood flowing. After this operation, they cleaned my head. When they finished doing all this, they gave me an appointment.

After three months, in a dream, I saw them coming back and intervening in the same way. They gave me a second appointment, and they did the same intervention. They gave me a third appointment; this time, they opened my head and washed it. At the end of this operation, they closed my head, healed me, and told me: "Go work for God."

The Third Intervention

For my third healing, God performed at the level of one of my eyes (the left eye). A speck in the shape of the letter T appeared in one of my eyes. While praying on a mountain, I held this T in my hand in broad daylight and began to pray, to praise God. God, in His love, cast His healing gaze upon me, and this T disappeared. This is how my third healing was done.

The Fourth Intervention

The fourth miraculous intervention that God granted me is dental healing. All my teeth were rotten, and I could not eat anything. I suffered, and in my pain, I said, "O God, it is not possible for me to be your servant and to be prey to this dental pain." In a dream, I saw someone giving me a little water and asking me to shake it in my mouth once, all the teeth fell into a white basin. The person asked me to do it a second and a third time, and all the teeth became normal. This pain disappeared, and I have not suffered from toothache since.

> **THROUGH THE SACRIFICE OF THE CROSS, THROUGH THE DIVINE BLOOD OF THE BLESSED ETERNAL GOD, HE HEALED MY SOUL.**

Spiritual Healing

My miraculous healing was divine. God performed several healings in my life. The results were spiritual and physical. Through the sacrifice of the cross, through the divine blood of the blessed eternal God, He healed my soul. Thus, I can quote the psalmist: "He restores my soul. He leads me in the paths of righteousness for his name's sake" (Psalm 23:3).

By the grace of my Savior and Lord Jesus Christ, I am able to cry out loud and intelligibly:

The LORD preserves the simple;I was brought low, and He saved me. Return to your rest, O my soul, For the Lord has dealt bountifully with you. —Psalm 116:6-7

Therefore, there is no condemnation for me, Wiljean Compère, who is in Christ Jesus. Indeed, the law of the Spirit who gives life in Christ Jesus has set me free from the law of sin and death (Romans 8:1).

My life is a life of miracles. God performed miraculous healings in my life. I give glory to God, who cast His healing gaze upon me in order to make me enjoy miraculous healings. This experience has allowed me to realize the importance of faith and perseverance in prayer. A section is dedicated to discussing this.

THE IMPORTANCE OF FAITH AND PERSEVERANCE IN PRAYER

A powerful prayer life requires unwavering faith and strong perseverance. It is written in the Bible:

The prayer of faith will save the sick. . . . Elijah was a man with a nature like ours, and he prayed earnestly that it would not rain, and it did not rain on the land for three years and six months. —James 5:15a, 17

Elijah was like us; his faith in the power of God prompted him to pray a prayer that made him witness the mighty hand of the Most High in action.

The demonstration of Jesus Christ to His disciples when He addressed them with a parable to teach them that they "always ought to pray and not lose heart" (Luke 18:1), and the salutary advice that the Holy Spirit entrusted to Paul for the Thessalonians by suggesting they pray without ceasing (1 Thessalonians 5:17) highlight the importance of perseverance in prayer.

The Prayer of Faith

Prayer—Prayer is a request by the Spirit made to God in the name of Jesus Christ in order to manifest the glory of God. It is a supplication aimed at fulfilling the divine will. The Bible states: "In everything, by prayer and supplication with thanksgiving, let your requests be made known to God" (Philippians 4:6b).

We find this statement in the Bible: "Pray . . . always with all prayer and supplication in the Spirit" (Ephesians 6:18a). A prayer made in the Spirit is a prayer that is in line with the will of God; such a prayer addressed to God in the name of Jesus (John 14:14) will result in a powerful outcome. Jesus declares: "Whatever you ask the Father in My name He may give you" (John 15:16b).

And all this is so that the name of God may be sanctified, and His will may be done on earth as it is in heaven (Matthew 6:9b-10). But by what means should the prayer we address to God be made?

Faith—This prayer must be made in faith. God wants us to present our prayers to Him at all times, and He requires it to be done with faith; otherwise, it will not have an effective result (James 1:6-8).

The Bible states: "Now faith is the substance of things hoped for, the evidence of things not seen" (Hebrews 11:1) and, "Without faith *it is* impossible to please *Him,* for he who comes to God must believe that He is, and *that* He is a rewarder of those who diligently seek Him" (Hebrews 11:6).

> FAITH REQUIRES ACTION; SOMETIMES, IT DEMANDS THAT WE MAKE A DECLARATION TO REMAIN SILENT TO CONTEMPLATE THE POWER OF GOD.

The woman who suffered from bleeding for twelve years was seeking a solution to her illness; her approach was filled with faith. She had the firm conviction that if she touched Jesus, she would be healed, and that's what she did to materialize her faith in Christ.

Faith requires action; sometimes, it demands that we make a declaration to remain silent to contemplate the power of God. Jesus said to the woman: "Your faith has made you well" (Matthew 9:22). And she was healed instantly.

The Prayer of Faith—The prayer of faith can mean considering what Jesus affirmed: "Therefore I say to you, whatever things you ask when you pray, believe that you receive *them,* and you will have *them*" (Mark 11:24).

Praying with Persistence—Praying with persistence can be defined as urgent prayer. The strength that leads to persistent prayer comes from faith strengthened by obedience to the Word of God.

The Bible declares that Elijah was a man with a nature like ours, and the fact that God listened to his prayer proved that he walked with, feared, and had an intimate relationship with God. He knew that God is a faithful God who always keeps His word and is compassionate and concerned about the needs of His children. All of this led him to approach *Jehovah-Jireh* without embarrassment or hesitation because he knew in whom he trusted and to whom he addressed his fervent request.

> WE MUST HAVE UNWAVERING FAITH IN GOD AND PERSEVERE IN THIS FAITH. IT IS THEN THAT WE EXPERIENCE A PRAYERFUL LIFE.

When we obey the divine voice, we present a sweet-smelling offering to God. From there, we put Him to the test. In His Word, God suggests: "And try Me now in this. . . . If I will not open for you the windows of heaven And pour out for you *such* blessing That *there will* not *be room* enough *to receive it* (Malachi 3:10b).

Faith and perseverance are the two important keys of the Christian warrior. This shows our love for God, the One who is worthy of our faith and in whom we trust, and the One for whom we must have a life of continual obedience and whom we must obey. We must have unwavering faith in God and persevere in this faith. It is then that we experience a prayerful life. He endowed me with this prayerful life on the mountain, in the prayer vigils.

So, I found myself in a spiritual battle; I had to take up these spiritual weapons: the sword of the Spirit being the Word of God and prayer. These weapons are offensive and defensive; they are powerful because the Word of God affirms: "The weapons we fight with are not the weapons of the world. On the contrary, they have divine power to demolish strongholds" (2 Corinthians 10:4, NIV).

God chose me, He healed me from my spiritual and physical illnesses. He called me. After much resistance, I answered Him, and He entrusted me with a mission to fulfill. I am willing to let myself be used by my God and Savior, Jesus Christ, because I find grace, a new nature, and a mission in Him. The Word of God declares:

For it is by grace you have been saved, through faith—and this is not from yourselves, it is the gift of God—not by works, so that no one can boast. For we are God's handiwork, created in Christ Jesus to do good works, which God prepared in advance for us to do. —Ephesians 2:8-10 (NIV)

CHAPTER 3

My Calling and Vocation

CALLING AND VOCATION

Calling and vocation are two complementary realities. Calling, being a request to come, precedes vocation. If one is called, they will be entrusted with a task to accomplish, which is the vocation.

Definition of "Calling"

A calling is an invitation issued comprehensibly, either by voice or gesture, to a person or animal for the purpose of coming.

Definition of "Vocation"

A vocation is the reason for which the invitation was issued. It refers to a specific responsibility to be carried out with the authority received from the one entrusting the responsibility.

God called Moses, saying, "Moses! Moses!" and he said, "Here I am" (Exodus 3:4b). God revealed His identity to him (Exodus 3:6) and presented the reason for calling him (Exodus 3:7-9).

In Exodus 3:10, God said to him, "Come now, therefore, and I will send you to Pharaoh." Here, God grants authority to Moses. Then He says, "You may bring My people, the children of Israel, out of Egypt." This is the vocation, the mission that God wanted Moses to accomplish.

Therefore, calling is a comprehensible request to come, while vocation is a mission given with the authority received in connection with the issued invitation.

God redeemed me by the divine blood of His only Son. In Him, He gave me a new identity: child of God, child of Light. He called me, and after being healed spiritually and physically by Him, He entrusted me with a mission.

> **CALLING IS A COMPREHENSIBLE REQUEST TO COME, WHILE VOCATION IS A MISSION GIVEN WITH THE AUTHORITY RECEIVED IN CONNECTION WITH THE ISSUED INVITATION.**

MY CALLING

My calling bears some resemblance to that of Abraham. God asked Abraham to leave his country to go to the unknown, and Abraham responded to the divine voice and went. God asked me to leave my city, my department, to go to the North department, but where exactly I should go, I did not know. However, I responded positively to the divine call.

From ninth grade on, God was calling me, but I refused because studying theology to engage in ecclesiastical activities meant choosing poverty. I did not want to be a pastor because I saw the harsh situation of pastors in my community. Instead, I preferred to be a great doctor, a renowned agronomist. But the Bible affirms, "Man proposes, God disposes." I am talking about my calling, but how did I receive it from God?

Following the healing dream in which God operated on my head, God told me, "Go work for God." It was the first time that God called me in a particular way. He would continue to call me, and this time He would convince me through this reminder.

It was during a prayer vigil at Madame Faublas Rafino's that God reminded me. During this prayer vigil, a voice resonated in my ears, and I heard these words, "I await you in the North."

The first time God called me, I wondered exactly what I should do and where. In this reminder, He gave me an appointment: I await you—but in what place?—in the North.

At the same time, I had a spiritual song that I sang, it was the lyrics of song number 65 in the French sections of the *Chant d'Espérance* hymnbook, which I want to share with you:

> *Jesus, by Your precious blood,*
> *Remove my iniquity!*
> *Look at me from heaven above,*
> *Your love has forgiven me everything.*
> *I wandered for a long time, my heart rebellious,*
> *But I hear Your voice calling me*
> *To the foot of Your cross, now,*
> *All confused, broken, I surrender.*
> *White, whiter than snow,*
> *Washed in the blood of the Lamb,*
> *I will be whiter than snow!*

Through this word from God, "I await you in the North," I was convinced that it was God who was calling me, and I had a strong desire to respond to this call, and the only way to do so was to go meet my God who calls me and awaits me.

Although I did not know exactly where I should go, I wanted to go to the North, even though it was an area where, at that time, I had neither family nor friends. At that time, I was in Plateau Central in the Centre department. I contacted my sister Roselie Compère to tell her that God was calling me and He wanted me to go to the North. Sister Roselie encouraged me to accept Jesus Christ as my Savior and Lord. When I shared this initiative with her, she thought I was struck with madness since I had no family in the North. But my decision was unchanged.

MY CALLING AND VOCATION   39

Without my parents' knowledge, I headed north. At that time, a missionary, the late Mrs. Anne-Marie Sully, came to organize a quarantine at the Church of God in Hinche. She gave me a suitcase, toiletries, a Scofield Bible, another Bible entitled the Deciphered Bible, and she said, go. She also gave me some money.

For the journey, Madame Faublas Rafino paid for my ride from Hinche to Pignon. Upon arriving in Pignon, I had to walk for two hours from Pignon to St-Raphaël. From there, a family, one of whose members made the journey with me without my knowledge, allowed me to spend the night under their roof.

Around 2:00 am, I got up; it was September 27, 1989, and a bus transported me to Cap-Haïtien, and I arrived at this destination at 6:30 am. Now, I was in the North, with no one coming to meet me, not knowing where I should go. Being at the bus station in Cap-Haïtien, a gentleman bought me something to eat (a snack); then he took me to Radio 4VEH, in Vaudreuil.

> **WHEN GOD CALLS A PERSON, HE NEVER PROMISES THAT EVERYTHING WILL BE WITHOUT DIFFICULTY, BUT HE PROMISES TO BE WITH US EVERY DAY.**

All of this allowed me to better understand the call that God issued to me by saying, "I await you in the North," through this gentleman, God welcomed me and provided me with food as He provided me with provisions for the journey because when

God calls His servant, He does not leave him orphaned. He is always there by his side, and His presence provides His servant with what he needs.

MY CALLING, DIFFICULTIES, AND DIVINE HELP

When God calls a person, He never promises that everything will be without difficulty, but He promises to be with us every day. He promises to come to our aid in times of distress when we share our plight with Him.

Upon arriving at Radio 4VEH, there were many people in the reception area. Among them, the late Mrs. Louis Destiné. She received me. Then, I was taken to the Bible school, which later became Emmaus Bible Seminary. It became a seminary with my class.

On a Monday, September 27, 1989, Mr. David Dicky took me to Emmaus Bible Seminary for an admission assessment. In the examination, we were given a sentence and asked to identify the type of complement in the sentence. David also participated in this admission assessment; he asked me to give him the answer to this question. I did not want to give it to him, but I did so later.

At the end of this evaluation, David asked me, "Where do you live?" I replied that I did not have a home; I did not know. During this time, I found myself in front of the gate of OMS International at 4VEH without knowing where to go. So, David said to me, "Since you have no place to stay, come to my place; I have a small bed you can sleep on." When I arrived at his house, he asked his parents if there was a possibility to accommodate me since I had no home. Indeed, his mother agreed to receive me into her home.

The housing problem was solved. But another problem arose; I was Pentecostal while David was Baptist. The tendencies of these two denominations do not agree on all points. But we found an agreement, although there were points on which we did not agree.

Since I successfully passed the admission exam, I was accepted as a student at Emmaus Bible Seminary. But I only had fifty cents. I was dependent on the family that received me for my food because I had nothing substantial to offer. Consequently, I was poorly fed. The situation seemed a bit difficult for me.

Despite everything, I continued to study. One Friday, aware of my difficult situation, I prayed to God, saying, "Lord, it is not possible for me to have no house to stay in; if you truly call me, allow there to be an open door before me so that I can enter freely."

At the end of the week, the dean, whose name was Steve, an Englishman, asked me: Where do you live? I replied that I had no home to live in. Then he replied, "If you have no housing, how will you be able to continue with your studies?"

At that time, there were no dormitories in the seminary. So the dean called Mrs. Louis Destiné to tell her that a student had no home to stay in and asked if she could help. Considering the situation, Mrs.

Louis Destiné called Mrs. Dieu-Grand Étienne to ask her if she had a room to rent to accommodate a student.

Mrs. Dieu-Grand found a room, but I had no money to pay the rent. So, since Mrs. Dieu-Grand was the servant of Mrs. Clane Beauman, she told her that there was a student who had no home to live in during his study cycle. A room to rent had been found, but he had no money to pay the rent. In fact, Mrs. Clane Beauman decided to pay for me, and Mrs. Louis Destiné took responsibility for giving me money for food. Upon arriving in the room, there was nothing, not even a chair. Then a nurse named Miss Éveline Saint-Fleur gave me a small bed, and Mrs. Dieu-Grand bought me a mattress.

God provided for my needs through His servants. For my accommodation and food, everything was settled. But there was another problem; I had no money to pay for tuition. I was called to the dean's office of the seminary for tuition fees and asked to settle my debt. I told the members of the dean's office that God told me that He would open a door before me, according to Revelation 3:8. The door was not yet open, so I waited to see what He would do since it was He who sent me.

The following week, the dean's office called me to say that if I did not pay the tuition fees, I would not be considered a student of the seminary. In an attempt to solve this problem, a meeting convened, and the dean's office said they could not accept me because I had no money to pay my debt. I told them that the door was not yet open. Therefore, I could do nothing.

> **DESPITE THE SADNESS THAT FILLED MY HEART, I DID NOT LOSE HOPE BECAUSE THE LORD WAS MY SHEPHERD, AND I WOULD NOT WANT (PSALM 23:1).**

They gave me time to settle this debt. However, Dean Steve did not want me to be dismissed because he had great regard for me because of my good grades in class. However, there was a law that required payment for tuition fees.

Faced with this difficult situation, I shed tears. But despite the sadness that filled my heart, I did not lose hope because the Lord was my shepherd, and I would not want (Psalm 23:1). So I addressed the God who provides, who is faithful to fulfill promises, and I said, "Lord, what should I do, for I will be dismissed?" After praying to God, I contacted Mrs. Dieu-Grand and informed her of my situation.

Since there were children with whom she worked, she asked me to work with them, and she said to me, "If you are useful to God, He will act in your favor so that you can continue with your studies." While I was working with the children, there was a missionary who came from Canada; he was passing through the area where I was working with the children, it was Beatty Barbara Maclean. In the meantime, I was singing with the children this little chorus in Creole:

David is a big man.
He rose to dance.

When the Ark entered the land of Israel,
He rose to dance
And praised the Lord.
Praise, praise, praise the Lord.
He rose to dance and praised the Lord.

The missionary, Bity Barbara Mackline, was listening to me sing; he asked those around him, "Who is singing like this?" They told him that it was a student who had neither clothes, shelter, nor money to pay his tuition; that's why he sings like that.

As they spoke, the people talking with the missionary thought they were worsening my situation; however, they were working in my favor.

So, the missionary asked them: "Where does he study?"

They replied that I was a student at Emmaus Bible Seminary.

He responded: "You say he has nothing?"

Then Bity Barbara Mackline went to the dean's office of the seminary. He paid for my four years of theological studies.

Upon my return to the seminary the following week, the dean called me to the office and asked me: "Do you know that someone is paying for one month for you?" I said I did not know. At that time, he told me: "Mr. Wiljean, since you had no money to pay the tuition, we were going to dismiss you, but there was someone who paid for one month for you; you can go to your class; we will bring you the payment slip."

I continued to study with a heart full of peace because God paid for this study cycle for me. I still got good grades. At the end of this cycle, I graduated with a degree. I did my internships at the Evangelical Church of Vaudreuil, the Wesleyan Church of Borgne. Later, I continued my studies for a bachelor's degree and graduated at the end.

But Bity Barbara Mackline made a demand of me, saying, "I paid for your study cycle, so promise me that you will not leave Haiti. You must stay in Haiti to work to help your country because that is why I paid for your education."

Indeed, I hold this commitment dear to my heart. That is why I engage in work by providing support where it is needed. And that is one of the reasons why I never want to leave Haiti.

Thus, God cleared the path under my steps to advance on the path He prepared for me in order to manifest His glory in my life because He heard my cries; He saw my tears. By His infinite love, He received me in His paternal arms, consoling me with His perfect joy.

> **WHEN GOD IS IN CONTROL OF YOUR SITUATION, DO NOT LET DOUBT WEAKEN YOUR FAITH, BUT REMAIN CALM, LET YOUR FAITH BE ROOTED IN GOD'S REDEEMING STRENGTH, AND AFTERWARD, YOU WILL SEE THE MANIFESTATION OF HIS ALMIGHTY POWER IN YOUR FAVOR.**

God always keeps His promises; He never forgets His children in distress; through His triumphant arms, He always brings them help at the right time. With God, there is always hope, even in the most difficult times. You who are discouraged at the sight of life's storms, I want to tell you that in Jesus Christ, you can find a rampart; in Him, you can find a suitable solution to your needs.

It is important to know that when God is in control of your situation, do not let doubt weaken your faith, but remain calm, let your faith be rooted in God's redeeming strength, and afterward, you will see the manifestation of His almighty power in your favor. Faced with difficulties for which I could not provide a solution, I firmly awaited the help of my God, who promised to open a door that no one could close. God watches over His Word to fulfill it, for He is a faithful God (Jeremiah 1:12).

So God made me understand by His actions in my favor that He does not leave me orphaned, for He came to my aid. Thus, I would like to share a verse of this very significant song, which is found in number 310 of *Chants d'Espérance* French section:

Without waiting, I want to strive
For the promised happiness;
Whoever leaps, whoever advances
Will obtain the prize.
I am a child of my God,
And it is He who defends me.
So, let's go! No doubt
The goal is so great.

Now, my studies had come to an end, but I wanted to earn a master's degree in theology in the United States. While I was dreaming, a person came to me and said, "Wiljean: I did not call you only to study; I also have ministries that I want you to carry out for me in Haiti." I understood that it was God speaking to me.

Indeed, I understood that God wanted me to engage in ministry, so I devoted myself to prayer for three months to know what God wanted me to do and where He wanted me to exercise the ministry He would entrust to me.

MY VOCATION

When God calls a person, He always has a mission that He wants that person to accomplish for His glory and for the advancement of His work on earth in order to meet the needs of weary and burdened hearts. God wants man to seek God's kingdom and righteousness first; all other things will be given to him thereafter (Matthew 6:33).

As for the vocation God entrusted to me, God asked me to work for Him in an abandoned garden so that it could bear fruit. This was revealed to me in a dream after my theological studies.

Upon receiving God's call and vocation, I engaged in prayer to know exactly where God wants me to work for Him. Since He called me and entrusted me with this mission, He showed me the place where I should work for Him while reassuring me of His presence, which is why He gave me the authority to accomplish the mission He entrusted to me.

In this section, we will shed light on how God entrusted me with the mission, how I located the community in which God wanted me to exercise the ministry entrusted to my humble person and my family's involvement in the ministry. In the following lines, you will continue to see how God repairs breaches and manifests His glory to those who believe in His Word and obey Him.

ENTRUSTED WITH A MISSION

To try to pave the way to delve directly into the subject of this section, which is how God informed me of the vocation He wants me to fulfill for Him, let's take an approach to the calls and vocations that occur in Acts chapter 9.

THE CALL AND VOCATION OF SAUL AND ANANIAS

Acts 9 presents the conversion of Saul, who later became known as Paul. In his conversion, we find his call and vocation, and we can also observe the call and vocation of Ananias.

The Call and Vocation of Paul

Here is what is written in the Word of God regarding his call:

Suddenly a light shone around him from heaven. Then he fell to the ground, and heard a voice saying to him, "Saul, Saul, why are you persecuting Me?" And he said, "Who are You, Lord?" Then the Lord said, "I am Jesus, whom you are persecuting. . . ." So he, trembling and astonished, said, "Lord, what do You want me to do?" —Acts 9:3-6

This passage presents Paul, his call, and his response to the divine call with two very significant questions: "Who are you, Lord?" and "Lord, what do you want me to do?"

The Lord gives him two very special answers that allow Paul to know first with whom he is dealing: "I am Jesus," the self-sufficient One, the One who exists by His own power. Otherwise, I am the God-Savior. And then, to be aware of his state of sin: "Whom you are persecuting?" Although he persecutes Jesus, Jesus calls him because He is the God-Savior, and His mission is to seek and save the lost (Luke 19:10). And the other answer is this: "Get up, go into the city, and you will be told what you must do." In this part, we find Paul's mission but veiled.

The Call and Vocation of Ananias

In verses 10 and 14 of this chapter, we find the call and vocation of Ananias and the pretext that reflects the reality of Moses in Exodus 3 when he hears the call and vocation of God entrusted to him. The call and vocation of Ananias have a crucial importance for the vocation of Paul because it is Ananias whom God will use to allow Paul to know it.

The call and vocation of Ananias are given in a vision when the Lord called him by name and gave him information about where exactly Saul of Tarsus was, and God also informed Saul of Tarsus about the special visit that Ananias would pay him in a vision.

In this spiritual work, God informs both Ananias and Saul of Tarsus. Indeed, both can be convinced that it is God who is acting. Here, we find a spiritual lesson whose application in ministry is of paramount importance in order to be at the center of God's will. It is evident that there should be no confusion, no doubt about what God wants to accomplish through the lives of His servants for the fulfillment of His purposes. God shows us that this must be done in prayer.

Despite the evidence given by God, Ananias presents pretexts for not going to Saul of Tarsus. Thus, God asks him to go and share with Saul the vocation that God entrusts to him for His servant:

But the Lord said to him, "Go, for he is a chosen vessel of Mine to bear My name before Gentiles, kings, and the children of Israel. For I will show him how many things he must suffer for My name's sake." —Acts 9:15-16

Verses 17 and 18 of this chapter clarify Ananias's obedience to God's command and the fulfillment of his vocation; he said to Saul of Tarsus:

> *"Jesus, who appeared to you on the road as you came, has sent me that you may receive your sight and be filled with the Holy Spirit." Immediately there fell from his eyes something like scales, and he received his sight at once.*

Meanwhile, let us directly address the subject of this section: The way God entrusted me with the mission.

To know what God wanted me to do, after completing my theological studies, I spent three months in prayer because I wanted to know what God wanted me to do as a ministry, whether my vocation was to be a teacher, evangelist, or pastor. After three months, God revealed to me what He wanted me to do. I wanted to return to Cerca Carvajal to work in my church, but it was not God's will.

In a dream, God told me that there was a ministry He wanted me to accomplish for Him in Cap-Haïtien. There, I found myself at the foot of a mountain, in front of an abandoned garden whose Owner claimed that He had never eaten its fruit. Then, He said to me: "Wiljean, can you cultivate this garden for Me?"

I replied, "No, I cannot cultivate it."

He said to me, "You can cultivate it because I will be with you."

I replied saying, "This garden cannot produce anything to eat, and then you ask me to take care of it?"

He said, "Yes, this time, I would like to eat the fruit of this garden because I will be with you."

I saw the garden, a large garden of peas and corn. In the end, I agreed to work the garden. After the Owner finished entrusting me with the responsibility of cultivating this garden, at the same moment, I started to hoe, clean, and plant corn and peas. At that moment, the seeds began to sprout. Then the Owner said to me, "Good job; do not be afraid, for I am with you."

Indeed, this was the calling that God had addressed to me, asking me to cultivate for Him the abandoned garden and the authority He had given me by telling me not to be afraid, for He was with me. He had guaranteed me that He would eat the fruit of this garden through me. All of this happened in a dream.

Upon waking up, there was a mountain where I used to fast called Bethany. After spending a moment of prayer on this mountain, asking God to show me the location of the garden He wanted me to cultivate for Him, I descended from the mountain. Then, I went to see a friend named Eutrope Samson with the intention of explaining to him what I saw in the dream. I told him that in the dream, I saw myself at the foot of the mountain of Milot, about to enter Limonade. At that time, a landowner asked me to cultivate an abandoned garden which he had never eaten from, and he wanted me to cultivate this garden so that he could eat its fruit. Eutrope Samson told me that what I saw in the dream was a church that used to function but had been closed seven years ago. God wanted me to restore this church.

After receiving this news through Eutrope's explanation, I was deeply moved because I had barely finished my theological studies with great difficulty, and on top of that, I only had fifty cents. God was asking me to restore this church. I was not under the cover of any mission, and I was not affiliated with any church. I was afraid to take on this responsibility.

This church had been under the leadership of the late Pastor Méhu Louis. It was located in Bas-de-Lance, Limonade. Since Eutrope couldn't go with me, I returned to the mountain of Bethany to continue praying to God. I said to God in my prayer, "Lord, show me where this church is."

After finishing praying, I descended from the mountain to go to Cap-Haïtien. There, there was a driver going to Cap-Haïtien, so I asked him if I could go with him because I didn't have money to pay for transportation.

He asked me, "Who are you?"

I replied, "I am Pastor Wiljean Compère."

He asked, "You are a pastor; where is the church you lead?"

I told him that I had just finished my theological studies, so I was waiting for God to send me where He wanted me to work for Him.

The driver told me that he had a church he could give to me. He said he was doing business in Bas-de-Lance. There was a church where pharmaceutical and food products were sold. It had become a market because it had been closed for seven years. It broke my heart to see the precarious situation of this church. Since he said he could give me this church, I asked him if he had a mission. He said he didn't have a mission, but as a Christian, the situation of this church saddened him a lot.

Arriving in Cap-Haïtien, since I had to leave him, he said to me, "Pastor Wiljean, I beg you. I encourage you to go and restore this church."

I didn't know the driver, but he was like an angel of God guiding me. I never saw him again. I had no information about him. Afterward, as a theme, the expression "Bas-de-Lance de Limonade" kept coming to my mind from time to time.

Aware of the importance of this recurring theme, I dedicated myself to praying about it. Since I didn't know exactly where Bas-de-Lance was, I tried to find someone who could help me locate it. I lived in Vaudreuil, and to go to this area, one had to go through Cap-Haïtien, Quartier-Morin, Limonade, to reach Bas-de-Lance. But I must say that I did not yet know these areas perfectly. I only had information.

So, I was talking about this subject with a friend named Joe Waters, an American with a damaged hand who used to visit Haiti. He told me that he would buy me a bicycle.

I rode from Vaudreuil to Bois-de-Lance on this bicycle. This journey could take two hours. Along the way, I asked people I met, "Please: Where is Bois-de-Lance?"

Interestingly, Joe Waters, the American friend I was talking to about this subject, came from an Open Door Church of God. So, God asked me to restore a church that I would name Open Door. In my opinion, my meeting with Joe Waters was confirmation. God allowed Joe Waters to give me a bicycle with which I traveled from Cap-Haïtien to Limonade, specifically to Bas-de-Lance.

Arriving in Bas-de-Lance, it was a Saturday, a market day, the vendors came to sell their food and pharmaceutical products. Being in this place, I looked up and saw a sign: National Baptist Church. This church had been closed for seven years.

From there, I heard a voice saying to me: "Stop, you have arrived!"

Truly, I stopped; then I engaged in a conversation with those around me. They confirmed to me that this church was led by the late Pastor Méhu Louis. In the meantime, I entered the church; inside, there were people selling and eating, as it had become a market. At that moment, I heard the voice of God saying to me: "You can start working, for it is this garden that I asked you to cultivate for Me so that I may eat its fruit." At that very moment, I committed to work by surveying the area.

I found a man in the churchyard named Augusma Prédestin, a voodoo priest who lived in a small house with his family. He told me he came to accept Jesus Christ as Savior and Lord. Then, Augusma told me, "The person in charge of this land is the son of the late Pastor Méhu Louis; it has been a long time since he visited this land, but you can work. When he comes, you can talk to him about this land."

It was Saturday, September 20, 1993. That same day, I started working. But don't forget that I only had fifty cents because God called me to leave my city and my neighborhood to go to the North. It was with this money that I started this ministry. So, I took the initiative to live in this community. I committed myself to preaching the Gospel of Christ.

There were three comrades who appreciated the way I preached while I was at the seminary; they were Pastor Délitien Lecifort, Désamour Frandy, and Brother Pierre Délius, who came to Christ through my ministry, and I baptized him. He intended to enter the seminary to become a priest. By accepting Jesus Christ as Savior and Lord, he left everything to serve the Lord. I gave him a letter of recommendation to enter the Faculty of Theology of the Christian University of Northern Haiti, Limbé. After these four years of theological studies, he returned to the Open Door ministry to work. Later on, he became a pastor. This pastor left his house and his family to live with me and Augusma Prédestin. He said that if he were to enter the ministry, it would be in collaboration with Pastor Wiljean Compère. Now, he is not only an associate pastor of the Open Door Church of God in Bas-de-Lance but also the general secretary of the Open Door Biblical Seminary of

Bas-de-Lance. We continued to work to evangelize for a period of three months.

> ## DESPITE THE TRIALS, GOD PROVIDED FOR THE NEEDS OF HIS CHURCH SO THAT IT COULD DEVELOP FOR HIS GLORY.

During preaching and evangelistic campaigns, many young people came to Christ. The church began to grow but did not have chairs or benches. During this time, we suffered from hunger. From time to time, I had to go to Vaudreuil to get something to eat, a few pots of rice and wheat. Despite everything, God allowed His church to gather, and God allowed us to make some benches, but it must be said that the roof of the church was not in good condition.

Since there were people selling pharmaceutical and food products, we asked them to stop these commercial activities in this place, telling them that God was now restoring His church. Despite the trials, God provided for the needs of His church so that it could develop for His glory.

The Open Door Church of God began to grow, and many people converted to Christ. However, the voodoo priests continued with their voodoo ceremonies and with much arrogance. They interrogated me and asked me to leave the area, telling me that this area did not belong to me; it belonged to them.

During a period of four years, we engaged in a series of evangelistic campaigns and crusades. We did door-to-door evangelism. In the first crusade we organized, the preacher was Evangelist Saintilus Siméus. The preaching of the evangelist strongly impacted Mariolatry (doctrine on the veneration of Mary). From December 20, 1993, to September 27, 1999, the voodoo priests set fire to the temple of the Open Door Church of God numerous times.

When the Holy Spirit is at work, the evil one will not remain without reaction, although he cannot do anything to destroy the work of God. Through the voodoo priests, the evil one will react; one day, the voodoo priests set fire to the temple where the Open Door Church of God gathered, but that was not serious. On a Friday, seeing this, I began to glorify God because He did not allow this fire to destroy the temple where His church gathered.

But it did not end there, on a Thursday, which was September 27, 1999, the voodoo priests returned and completely set fire to the temple. I must tell you that I started my theological studies ten tears earlier on September 27, 1989. It was a terrible blow. But God did not leave us orphaned. Faced with this misadventure, my whole family and my wife asked me to leave the area because if they burned down the temple, they would have no fear of attacking me. On Friday, when I came to do the Bible study, all I saw was ashes.

To comfort me, a consoling voice spoke to me and said: "It's not you who was burned; it was the temple because it's not this burnt temple that is the church, but it's you. You don't need to be afraid, because

I told you that I am always with you. I told you that I will never abandon you. Therefore, your door is barely open, don't be afraid."

The police came and took statements. I was asked if I wanted to make arrests, but I said that God was the owner of His church. If someone set fire to the temple where His church gathered, it was up to God to defend His church. The Ministry of Worship, Justice, and the committee of the Open Door Church of God of Bas-de-Lance all wanted me to proceed with the arrest of the people involved in this unfortunate event, but no arrests were made. Moreover, I was sleeping at the time of the fire, so I did not know who was involved.

The temple was beautiful and well burnt, but the Open Door Church of God continued to worship the God of heaven and earth, the Almighty. In the churchyard, there is a mango tree. It was under this mango tree that the Open Door Church of God gathered for a year. Every day, we worshiped God under this mango tree, which we could consider a temple. The photo of this mango tree is inserted in this book. It continues to bear mangoes.

Despite everything, the Open Door Church of God continued to worship God with the limited means it had. But God would open a door for us; that is, God allowed me to receive an invitation to participate in a conference called Amsterdam 200, which was held under the direction of Billy Graham in Titanyen, Haiti. God allowed me to comment on this series of conferences.

Through this, He allowed me to travel for the first time. This can be explained in that not only did Evangelist Billy Graham invite me to participate in another conference held in Amsterdam, but also for the trip, he paid for everything for me. I traveled from New York to Miami without an American visa to go to Europe to participate in the Amsterdam 200 Conference. And everything went well by the grace of God. During this terrible period, it was one of the great things that God was able to accomplish for me.

Later, there was a major event that occurred while the Open Door Church of God was conducting an evangelistic campaign. There were about five voodoo priests who gathered and asked me to leave the Bas-de-Lance community. Among them was a voodoo priest named Zokoko; he told me that they bought the Bas-de-Lance community. Therefore, if I did not leave Bois-de-Lance, he would kill me and eat me. Faced with this threat, I trembled.

But God comforted me with His all-powerful Word of Romans 8:31, saying to me: "If God is for you, who can be against you?" Comforted by God, I spoke, placing my hand on Zokoko's shoulder, and I said to him, "If you do not convert, if you do not accept Christ as your Savior and Lord, very soon, you will die." I pushed him and left.

Fifteen days later, while I was preaching on a Sunday, I was told that Zokoko had died. Consequently, all the voodoo priests left the area. Thus, God allowed the Gospel of Christ to make its way into this community with power and authority.

> **THE TRIALS IN THE LIFE OF A CHRISTIAN DO NOT COME TO DESTROY HIS FAITH, BUT THEY COME TO MAKE THE FAITH OF THE CHRISTIAN STRONGER, WHICH IS WHY WE MUST ENDURE THEM WITH PATIENCE WHILE REMAINING ATTACHED TO GOD.**

In the time of James, Christians were subject to many trials, but the apostle encouraged them to consider trials as perfect joy, knowing that when they are subjected to various trials, the testing of their faith produced patience which leads to perfection and fulfillment, so that they may have all the blessings of God (James 1:2-3). The trials in the life of a Christian do not come to destroy his faith, but they come to make the faith of the Christian stronger, which is why we must endure them with patience while remaining attached to God. Thus, we will see that it is certain that God is a support, a help that never fails in distress (Psalm 46:1).

CHAPTER 4

A Companion for Ministry and Family

God has given me a family that loves Him, and this is a blessing for my ministry. They collaborate with me to fulfill the vocation that God has granted me.

THE NECESSITY OF A HELPER

The book of Genesis helps us understand that woman was created to be by man's side as a helpful wife and a significant collaborator, to support man in the responsibility that God entrusted to him. That's why God gave him a wife.

At that time, God asked me to get married, which was a very important matter because with this great responsibility, having a wife as a helper is of paramount importance. After seven years of ministry in the Bas-de-Lance community, God asked me to start a family. It seemed difficult to me because I did not have the means to meet the needs of my future family.

Since it was God who asked me to do so, even though I had neither money nor a house, I submitted to divine will. However, I had a great worry. This can be explained by the fact that I thought to myself that if God asked me to get married, how would I shoulder this responsibility to take care of my wife and family? But God's comforting voice reassured me, saying, "You have nothing to fear; I will take care of you as I did during your theological studies."

As for my economic resources, I had a savings account that my friend named Eutrope Samson had opened for me, but it contained only one thousand Haitian gourdes—about $8 US. I only had four thousand Haitian gourdes in total.

ENCOUNTERING MY FUTURE WIFE

On October 23, 1995, God allowed me to meet my future spouse. I courted her, and after two days, she responded on October 25, 1995. We engaged in a conversation for two days, Thursday and Friday. On Saturday, we gathered the necessary documents for the publication of our marriage banns. This took place at the Redford Baptist Church on a Sunday. Within eight days, I presented a sermon with Genesis 18 as the base text. The topic was "If you want to be blessed," and it had two points:
   1) Listen to God.
   2) Obey God.

Therefore, if you want to be blessed, it is not enough to hear or perceive God's voice as just a sound; you must listen to God's voice, understand what He has said to you, and not only listen but also obey God's voice because what you hear and apply will vitalize your faith.

Indeed, Jesus Christ said that if faith is active and powerful, it will show the glory of God (John 11:40). The one who can contemplate God's wonderful act is the one who demonstrates his faith by obeying God's voice; he is the one who will see the great way God acts. Thus, if you want to be blessed, you must listen to God's voice and obey God's Word.

While I was preaching this sermon, I asked the church to pray for me to find a spouse for marriage.

Indeed, God used me to preach this message, but in the end, I came to understand that it was directed at me because I did not want to marry Sister Jeannine Joliné because she was older than me. Yet, she was the one God wanted me to marry. It was disobedience on my part to God. Therefore, I listened to God's voice and obeyed Him by marrying Sister Jeannine Joliné. Accepting God's choice brought me many blessings.

Doing God's will is taking the path of blessing; even if the storm rages, never doubt God's faithfulness. He never despises anyone who submits to His Word.

After presenting this sermon, my future spouse came to thank me for the sermon. As she thanked me, I took some time to look at her. Then I left and went home. But in the evening, God spoke to me in a dream, saying, "The girl who thanked you after presenting your sermon, go find her and marry her, for she is the one I give you."

However, it is worth noting that one day, I approached Sister Jeannine Joliné Compère and said to her, "I am going to marry you."

She replied, "I am not your fiancé; how are you going to marry me?"

I retorted, "If you don't know it, then I will drop this project."

She added, "How are you going to marry a woman you do not love?"

I replied, "Over time, God will do it, but for now, I do not love you."

(I was right. I married her, and what is marvelous is that I love my wife passionately. I give glory to God for my wife; she is an important and blessed pillar within the Open Door ministry.)

MY MARRIAGE

Indeed, everything was done according to the will of God, and within a month and a half, God allowed us to marry. The ceremony of my marriage was extraordinary. God provided us with everything we needed. We had twenty-four godparents and twenty-four godmothers.

We did not yet have a house, but two people promised to give us one. A family appreciated the way I preached; the message that led them to appreciate me was titled, "If God Calls You, Get Your Feet Ready," and the text was John 4, concerning the story of the Samaritan woman. They decided to give us food. This family was the Mogène family. I engaged in intercession for Mrs. Atilor Mogène, so that she could have residency, as her husband was abroad. At that moment, she was granted her residency. She gave me the house where she lived to accommodate me and my family. Afterward, I asked my wife if she wanted to live in this house in Vaudreuil; she told me she did not because she was a teacher teaching in Milot. The commute would cost us a lot. She preferred to live in Cap-Haïtien, as her parents had a house there. Aware of our economic weakness, I agreed.

Then, her parents asked me if I agreed to live in their house. I did not enjoy this idea at first, but later on, I agreed. Living in my in-laws' house allowed me to be stable with my family. But from time to time, we would go to Bas-de-Lance to work in the ministry that God entrusted to us.

GOD'S CHOICE ALWAYS BRINGS GREAT BLESSINGS.

INTEGRATION OF MY FAMILY INTO THE MINISTRY

My entire family accompanies me in the exercise of my ministry. Sister Jeannine Joliné Compère is a pillar of utmost importance within the Open Door ministry. She is a woman of God, a woman of prayer. She supports me in everything I undertake. For me, she is a friend, an advisor, a collaborator. Her prayers have great value not only for the ministry but also for me. Hallelujah, God's choice always brings great blessings.

With the arrival of Sister Jeannine Joliné Compère in the Open Door ministry, God used her extraordinarily to advance this ministry in order to manifest His glory. My wife, she is a good helpmate for me. It is a divine grace to have her as a wife. The Bible is right to affirm:

> *Houses and riches are inherited from parents, but a prudent wife is from the Lord. . . . A virtuous wife is the crown of her husband. . . . He who finds a wife finds a good thing and obtains favor from the Lord. . . . Charm is deceitful and beauty is passing, but a woman who fears the Lord shall be praised. —Proverbs 19:14; 12:4a; 18:22; 31:30*

No one can succeed in their ministry without a wife given by God, a good wife. If my ministry is blessed, strong, and full of grace, it is because God is at work. She has strengthened me with her almighty power. He is always with me and I trust in Him. Yes, I believe in the Triune God, God the Father, the Son, and the Holy Spirit. He has given me a praying wife, submissive, obedient to the voice of God, and cooperative. And all this is because I submitted to the will of God.

After my trip to Amsterdam in 2000, we committed to building the church temple of the Open Door Church of Bas-de-Lance in 2001. God has allowed us to have a family of four: me, Pastor Wiljean Compère, Mrs. Wiljean Compère, our first child, a daughter, Wiljénie Compère, who is married to Mr. Judelin Jean Présumé, and our second child, a boy, Wiljerry Compère. He is engaged, and he will marry in a few years if God wills it. My whole family is dedicated to the service of the Lord Jesus Christ. It is a special grace. I give glory to God for this.

CHAPTER 5

The Impact of Open Door Ministry

The impact of Open Door ministry can be seen from various perspectives, as God has done wonderful things through this ministry to exercise His power for His glory and the advancement of His kingdom. The manifestation of the impact of Open Door ministry is seen spiritually, educationally, medically, financially, agriculturally, and in terms of livestock.

OPEN DOOR MINISTRY

Open Door ministry is a Christian, apolitical endeavor. It operates in the evangelical field to fulfill the missional mandate of Jesus Christ in Haiti and beyond (Matthew 28:18-20; Acts 1:8). It is committed to responding to the Great Commission of the Lord Jesus Christ with the help of the Holy Spirit in order to make positive impacts for the glory of God, the salvation of lost souls, the edification of the body of Christ, and the advancement of His kingdom. The greatest vision of Open Door ministry is to win Haiti for Christ. And God provides means for Open Door ministry to accomplish its work.

SPIRITUAL ACTIVITIES AT OPEN DOOR

For the edification of the body of Christ and the advancement of its work, various spiritual activities are carried out every year.

Children's Bible Camp

A children's Bible camp is organized every year for children from various departments of the country, different missions, and various churches. At this camp, Bible lessons are presented to children with the aim of strengthening their faith in Christ and attracting those who do not yet have Jesus Christ as their Savior and Lord. Throughout the camp, they participate in various activities. Devotions, games, and visits to cities and historical sites are organized for them, which is a great privilege for children living in rural areas. They eat together. At the end of this camp, a party is organized for them. During this camp, many children accept Jesus Christ as their Savior and Lord.

Annual Mission for Church Planting

An annual mission for church planting takes place every July, a work that is carried out with the participation of all the churches of Open Door ministry. Some churches may plant churches throughout the year.

Mission Deliverance in Trial

When God is at work, the evil one, even though he cannot prevent the work of God, still tries to do something. That is why the Bible invites us to submit to God and resist the devil, and he will flee from us (James 4).

The churches of Open Door ministry were on a mission to Magoyave with the purpose of planting a church in that community, as we do whenever we have missionary activities. After that, a group called Flamme Céleste from the Open Door Church of God in Cap-Haïtien took the initiative to return to this community to provide support to this young church. However, there was a very unfortunate incident, a tragedy that occurred. One of the sisters in this group died. This struck us with a great shock. The family greatly upset us with heated reactions and words. Transporting the deceased to the mortuary was not an easy task because this incident occurred in the countryside on a large mountain. The justice system intervened, and after an assessment, the deceased's family's lawyer demanded compensation for this family. But, a compromise was found.

The Open Door Church of God in Cap-Haïtien took on the responsibility of singing at our sister's funeral. We placed the deceased in the mortuary, and on the day of her funeral, we transported her to Camp-Coq. Leaders from the Open Door Church of God planned to go there to sing at the burial. What is important to note is that the deceased's family planned to harm the leaders, but God confused them by causing them to return the deceased to the mortuary, saying that it was not her time to die. But the funeral home did not accept her.

The police and the justice system intervened and checked to see if there was indeed a switch, and they saw that the name of the deceased was written under her feet. Indeed, it was her death. There was a man, a member of the deceased's family, who wanted to put me in prison; he was the one making fraudulent claims. But the justice of the peace and the police, after an investigation, put him in prison, and the deceased's family chose another mortuary for her. God was in control, and their plan failed.

> ## GOD DID NOT LEAVE US AS ORPHANS. HE GAVE US THE COURAGE TO OVERCOME.

In the end, the deceased's family sang at the funeral. God delivered me from this unfortunate event that could have caused the death of the leaders and increased my sorrow. In the midst of this distress, God did not leave us as orphans. He gave us the courage to overcome this tough trial. We spent around $85,000 for our sister's funeral. During this upheaval, the Open Door Church of God was in prayer; our God, who always hears the cries of His children, answered us with His comforting voice. That is why the Word of God affirms: "Call upon Me in the day of trouble; I will deliver you, and you shall glorify Me" (Psalm 50:15).

Annual Conventional Conferences
Every year, conventional conferences are organized for leaders of Open Door ministry in December to equip them for effective work of building up the churches and for the glory of God.

THE IMPACT OF OPEN DOOR MINISTRY
In this section, I want to emphasize the diverse realization of the mission that God has called me to accomplish because He has allowed Open Door ministry to grow and spread across several departments of the country. Within Open Door, one can clearly see God's hand through the institutions that have emerged from this Ministry. Open Door ministry is a blessed work comprising various institutions serving diverse purposes, all for the glory of God.

The institutions of Open Door ministry can be categorized as follows:

Open Door Churches
The Open Door ministry comprises thirty-three churches located in different areas of the country.

Churches in the Northern Department:
- Limonade (Bois-de-Lance)
- Limonade
- Cap-Haïtien
- Vaudreuil (Cap-Haïtien)
- Borgne (Péchaud)
- Pignon
- Pignon (Fontaine)

- Ranquitte (Savane Georges, Bas-Ranquitte)
- La Victoire
- Plaisance
- Acul du Nord (Grande Ravine)
- St Raphaël

Churches in the North-East Department:
- Fort-Liberté
- Ouanaminthe Zone 1
- Ouanaminthe Zone 2
- Trou du Nord
- Sainte-Suzanne
- Mombin Crochu (Logatte)

Church in the Artibonite Department:
- Gonaives
- Saint-Michel-de- l'attalaye

Churches in the Central Department:
- Hinche
- Magoyave (laboc)
- Maissade
- Bourouque (Maissade)
- Lacienne (Cerca Carvajal)
- Laborque (Cerca Carvajal)
- Colladere (Cerca Carvajal)

Church in the West Department:
- Port-au-Prince (Cité-Soleil)

Open Door Primary and Secondary Schools

In order to provide not only the Bread of Life but also the bread of education to the Haitian population, various schools are founded within several Open Door Churches in different departments. There are seven Open Door schools:
- Bois-de-Lance (Primary and Secondary)
- Ouanaminthe zone 2
- Cerca Carvajal
- Lacienne
- Acul-du-Nord, Grande Ravine
- Borgne, Péchaud
- La Victoire

Bas-de-Lance Health Center

The Open Door Health Center is a blessing to the Boisde-Lance community. It offers various services to this community, including hospitalization, maternity services, pediatrics, gynecology, and nutrition services. There is also a laboratory and other services. It operates 24/7.

Bas-de-Lance Open Door Bible Seminary

Before discussing the Open Door Seminary, it is important to mention the Porte Bible School. In the Porte Bible School, an effective program was presented to young male and female students to work with other young people in their churches. Our students were well received at various seminaries due to their training in this school. The Porte Bible School lasted from 2008 to 2017, a span of nine years.

Aware of the effectiveness of the training provided to the youth, we decided to establish a Bible seminary to continue with our students instead of leaving them with this training or providing other Bible seminaries. It was not mandatory for the students to stay with us, but they decided to continue their theological studies at the Open Door Bible Seminary.

Thus, the Open Door Bible Seminary was established. Already, three cohorts have graduated from this Bible seminary. The professors teaching at the Open Door Seminary are qualified; they are masters and doctors. There is a cafeteria that allows students to eat three times a day. A dean's office comprising competent and responsible personnel leads this seminary. With a welcoming campus, many people come from everywhere to organize camps, retreats, and weddings. It is a place of reference and preference, and the door of the Open Door Bible Seminary is always open.

Orphanage

The Open Door ministry is endowed with an orphanage that welcomes children and cares for them spiritually, nutritionally, educationally, and medically under the guidance of competent and caring leaders. These individuals are for them, affectionate, loving parents, but also strict.

This reduces the number of children abandoned in the streets and the number of children involved in acts of banditry. We want to have good citizens, so it is passionate about continuously mentoring children, and this is from all perspectives.

Microfinance Program
Through this economic activity, many members of the Open Door ministry engage in activities that can facilitate their financial lives while also providing loans.

GOD THE PROVIDER

In life's difficulties, struggles, and moments of scarcity, in suffering, fear, and despair, God only needs our firm faith to turn times of distress into times of joy, to bring water from the rock, to open the floodgates of heaven, and to pour out blessings upon us in abundance (Malachi 3:10).

When I received God's call and vocation, He asked me to leave my family, my city, and my department, namely the Centre, to go to the Nord department, where God called me to accomplish His work.

The Bible presents several servants whom God has called to accomplish His purposes, among whom I want to mention Abraham. God called Abram, who later became Abraham, saying to him, "Go from your country, your people and your father's household to the land I will show you" (Genesis 12:1, NIV). This verse speaks of a total self-renunciation on Abraham's part to trust in God and God alone, and that is what he did.

Then, God made great promises filled with blessings:
"I will make you into a great nation
And I will bless you;
I will make your name great

And you will be a blessing
I will bless those who bless you
And whoever curses you I will curse
And all peoples on earth will be blessed through you."
—Genesis 12:2-4 (NIV)

This is a total and perfect blessing. This passage emphasizes the formation of the people of Israel in the land of Egypt and the establishment of the nation of Israel in the Promised Land, the property God gave to Jacob's children. God granted great blessings to Abraham and conferred a great reputation upon him and renown. He was very rich economically, as he had much wealth; he was also rich spiritually, enjoying an intimate relationship with God, ranking among the three great patriarchs: Abraham, Isaac, and Jacob. To speak of His faithfulness, God presents Himself as the God of Abraham, Isaac, and Jacob, thus, the God of the covenant. Abraham was great before God and before men, and all of this was the work of God.

> **OUR TRUST IN GOD MANIFESTS OUR FAITH IN HIM, AS DOES OUR OBEDIENCE. FOR GENUINE FAITH IS CHARACTERIZED BY ACTS OF OBEDIENCE TO THE VOICE OF GOD.**

Abraham, leaving his country, moved with much wealth; but I, leaving my city, my department, had only fifty cents. But this does not prevent God from using me to accomplish great things because

God only needs a manifest faith in Him to manifest His glory. David's faith in God allowed him to confront Goliath and triumph over him. Those who do not hope in God only experience failure, shame, defeat, and regret, but whoever trusts in God will never be put to shame. The Word of God affirms that with God, we will do great things, and it is He who will crush our enemies (Psalm 108:13). It continues to declare: "For everyone born of God overcomes the world. This is the victory that has overcome the world, even our faith" (1 John 5:4, NIV). Glory to You, Lord Jesus Christ, for all our work is the accomplishment of Your almighty power.

It is important to emphasize that our trust in God manifests our faith in Him, as does our obedience. For genuine faith is characterized by acts of obedience to the voice of God. Abraham's faith led him to do God's will to go to the land God promised to show him. David's faith led him to confront Goliath. I had a firm conviction that God had called me and entrusted me, in my humble personality, with a mission, and that prompted me to take the direction God wanted me to take in order to do what He wanted me to do.

The widow of Zarephath had only a handful of flour in a jar and a little oil in a jug as her only means of survival for a short time, but her faith and obedience to the voice of God, heard through His servant Elijah, made her experience the great way in which the incomparable, true, and unique God acts, so that she had flour and oil in abundance (1 Kings 17:9-16).

By listening to God's call and accepting the vocation God addressed to me, God promised me that He would be with me and that He had placed an open door before me that no one can shut (Revelation 3:8). God, through His living and powerful Word, gave strength and life to my weak faith which becomes triumphant faith in the valley of the shadow of death.

All of this can be explained by the fact that despite having only fifty cents and despite various illnesses, economic difficulties, and attacks from the evil one, God was always in control of the situation in order to protect me, to help me, and to make great provisions in my favor. All glory belongs to God alone, for "He raises the poor from the dust and lifts the needy from the ash heap; He seats them with princes, with the princes of his people" (Psalm 113:7-8, NIV).

God has provided for my journey from Hinche to Cap-Haïtien, for my food and lodging, and for my theological studies, and He has allowed me to have a fruitful ministry through the help of the Holy Spirit for the advancement of Christ's work and for His glory. Without God, I could not, I cannot, I will not be able to do anything.

The providing God has done great things for me, and I do not want to refrain from praising the name of my God, the Lord of Hosts, the God of wonderful provisions. God has given me several vehicles through His servants for the Open Door ministry. God gave me a bicycle at the beginning of this ministry. With this bicycle, I traveled through four communes to get to Bois-de-Lance to work in the field God entrusted to me, which lasted for about two years. Later on, through Brother Wilbert Merzulus, God gave me a motorcycle I used for about two to three years. God used Brother Wilbert to ask me to give the motorcycle to a friend, and then he gave me an Isuzu Trooper. Eventually, this Isuzu Trooper broke down. After five years, through Brother Wilbert, God allowed me to receive a Toyota 4Runner.

A terrible incident occurred during a trip accompanied by some foreigners while we were in the 4Runner with them. At that moment, the 4Runner was at full speed, and one of the tires completely came off. It was moving at a high speed, jumping and hitting the roof of a gas tank and then bouncing onto a Toyota and damaging it. I thought we were going to die, but God is always a refuge and strength, a very present help in trouble (Psalm 46:1), and He was there to grant us His mighty help. Faced with this terrible event, the foreigners were amazed because we were saved narrowly, but there was nothing serious. After two years, God gave me a brand new machine; it was a Toyota Hilux, and it served for ten years.

I CAN DO ALL THINGS THROUGH THE STRENGTH OF THE TRIUNE GOD.

I talked with an American friend, Mark, a Community Christ Church (CCC) member, about this transportation problem. The late director of the international mission, Eric Hanson, planned with a friend to buy a new vehicle to give me as a gift, a Toyota

Land Cruiser, priced at $70,000 US. I had no money to do all this, but the God of heaven and earth and everything in it provided all these things for me for the exercise of His work. Whoever trusts in God walks and will walk triumphantly, for God will take care of him.

So, I can do all things through the strength of the triune God. I had only fifty cents, but God has done great things for me, for my family, and for my ministry, to the point that the amount is immeasurable. He is a providing God. "The Lord is good to those whose hope is in him, to the one who seeks him" (Lamentations 3:25, NIV).

Conclusion

Furthermore, God is the great repairer of breaches. He is the merciful God who does not remain angry forever. God's grace toward me is indescribable; his patience and His love for me are unparalleled. I did not seek Him, but He had a plan of happiness for me. He has made me the man I would not be without His abundant and precious grace. He has made me a repentant sinner. He has chosen me and used me for His glory.

Lost sinner that I was, He saved me from the condemnation of sin and death (Romans 8:2). He healed my soul. He changed my direction and my goals. He granted me the greatest good, the forgiveness of my sins. He performed various wonderful healings in my life for His glory at different times. His piercing and loving voice, merciful under the influence of the Holy Spirit, convinced me. I could not resist His powerful call. He called me to leave my family, my department, and my city and go north for His holy and righteous reason.

> **HE IS THE MERCIFUL GOD WHO DOES NOT REMAIN ANGRY FOREVER.**

In receiving the call of my God and following the direction to which God calls me, my family saw only folly in it because I am not from the north. We sing the words of song 156 in our collection of *Chants d'Espérance:* "He, who traces the road for worlds as for winds, will lead the steps of His children without fail." God did not leave me alone. He made provisions of all kinds for me through His servants.

> **GOD SHOWED HIMSELF TO BE THE GOD OF HEAVEN AND EARTH AND ALLOWED HIS CHURCH TO CONTINUE WITH THE TASK HE WANTED IT TO ACCOMPLISH.**

Despite economic difficulties, He allowed me to enter Emmaus Biblical Seminary to study theology in order to work for Him. Everything went well by the grace of God. After my studies, God called me to work for Him in Bas-de-Lance, my mission was to restore for Him a church that was abandoned. As He is the ultimate Shepherd, He allowed me to find His sheep, and thus He allowed His church, which He asked me to call Open Door Church, to be reborn.

Many oppositions and fires arose at the manifestation of the glory of God in this community, but God showed Himself to be the God of heaven and earth and allowed His church to continue with the task He wanted it to accomplish. I, who had only fifty cents, God allowed me to achieve great things in order to make positive impacts for the manifestation of His glory.

www.ingramcontent.com/pod-product-compliance
Lightning Source LLC
Chambersburg PA
CBHW062119080426
42734CB00012B/2919